by

Unleashed by P. G. Wodehouse

Grossman Publishers
A Division of The Viking Press
New York, 1974

Sir Crespi, One Way, Topper, Asta, Fala, King Mohegan, Angela, Perry, Hunter, Three Spot, Star, Dipper, Rocket, Nails, Charlie, Chance, Archie, Soda Pop, Mench, Flyer, Red, Bernie, Knee High, Smitty, Jeff, Gum Drop, Blackie, Esmarelda, Kehoe, Boojum, Champ, Schatz, Shamus, Jason, Gypsy, Jeana, Jamie, Homer, Rembrandt, Misnomer, Pal, Missy, Sluffy, Coony, Marty, Where-are-you, Cubby, Puppin, Cognac, Pluto, B. Baby, Lad, Rory, Damit, Albert, Victoria, Natasha, King Timahoe, Checkers, Balto, Snooper, Abercrombie, Star, Rocky, McTavish, McSam, Sunny, Woofie, Pong, Puffin, Samson, Chamois, Reddy, Herbie, Darius, Sop, Churchill, Toy, Tiger, Bear, Max, Frowl, Clarence, Kelly, Posie, Cosey, Hannibal, Chops, Bowser, Fritzie, Blackie, Jacob, Panchiti, Enuk, Jessie, Gaston, Gaspard, Toto, Sandy, RinTinTin, Maurice, Duchess, Lady, Shipupi, Skipper, Cleo, Angus, Waldo, Elmer, Ralph, Pixie, Daiquiri, Bullet, Jet, Spaghetti, Radar, Chip, Peanuts, Caboose, Bernard, Snoopy, Sebastian, Troubles, Pluto, Maggie, Gretchen, Chuck, Tramp, Nutka, L'Etoile, Shadow, King, Whitie, Lassie, Snowball, Dogonit, Thor, Wolfgang, Barnabus, Wag, Beelzebub, Trafalgar, Emma, Dickens, Winny, Mr. Jones, Josh, Bruce, Louie, Scotia, Arthur, Jordan, Sabrina, Samantha, Panda, Bushka, Baba, Sport, Bumble, Gaspacho, Percival, Duffy, Fool, Confucius, Nina, Ivan, Skooter, Andrew, Demi-tass, Beanie, Mut, Mike, Fergus, Raquel, BamBam, Nigel, Sheba, Taffy, Whiskey, Brandy, Krista, Cleo, Boliver, Lennie, Toodles, Tootsie, Cooch, Harry, Fritzie, Tenny, Trixie, Orestes, Louie, Sundance, Dona, Teppy, Hushy, Taffy, Curly, Mutsie, Ma, Ninety, Jetsy, Sammy, Shotsie, Cydney, Pasquel, Tory, Smokie, Whitney, Molly, Bobtail, Black Bart, Golly, Aikido, Saucy, Friday, Chopper, Mister Zipper, Shadow, Bozo, Griffin, Jiggsy, Queenie, Jeff, Munch, Lilly, Jason, Blue, Alice, Frisky, Socrates, Coco, Libby, Tibby, Bach, Jolie, Poupette, Blondie, Butter, Trixie, Laddie, Diana, Peppy, Taffy, Elsa, Pero, Meg... ...nberg, Chien D'Or, Partou, Boy, Mister, Cindy, Slipper, Cind... ...el, Hey You, DeGaulle, Maggie, Marquis, Lucky, Trigger, F... ...Pim, Brandt, Brownie, Daisy, Robespierre, Major, Penny,... ...ght, Red, Cookie, Tinker, Porkie, Tootsie, Binky, Ludwig, The... ...tty, Sarge, Henry, Cleo, Chan, Peppy, Ladybug, Nanette,... ...y Samantha, Rip, Oliver, Silky, Donovan, Hobo, Yofi, Nannie, Scratch, Sean, Suzie, Fella, Bingo, Yetti, Alex, Honey Boy III, Schnorkel, Bonnie, Gravy, Prudence, Réal, Mr. Wu, Dickens, Shadow, Sazzie, Cooch Popov, Mieza, Magot, Rosette, Semiramis, Coquinette, Flamenco, Lotus, Trompette, Fido, Kiki, Foutriquet, Vulcain, Tcholo, Tarzan, Arthur, Chat, Kelb, Coco, Jiggsy, Queenie, Jeff, Munch,

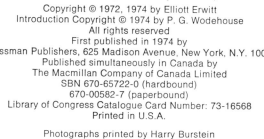

For Ellen, Misha, David, Jennifer, Geordie and their friends:

Pooch, Sweeney, Piper, Chang, Vickie, Daisy, Topsy, Dice, Muffett, Mr., Hoot, Soldier, Sambo,
Sam, Bosie, Doctor, Rosie, Lulu, Charlie, Skokie, Melvin, Tam, Chin, Colonel, Perky, Rebel,
Miura, Vodka, Harka, Arthur, Rover, Cooch, Sarah, Pooky, Bonny, Wow, Oliver, Kat, Muffy,
Gordon, Princess, Cassius-Emarud, Harvey, Beauregard, Lass, Charlie, Dude, Polonius,
Hamlet, Beowof, Heathcliff, Xenobia, Kuala, Pudo, Pudipu, Poochie, Snooky, Beno, Belly,
Hector, Ho-chi, Fred, Maggin, Pounceforth, Teobaldo, Mattatias, Terry, Igor, Lady, Frisky,
Cindy, Brutus, Beou, Moauer, Rex, Felix, Arthur, Missi, Cecilia, Randolph, Sadie, Smokey,
Hoot, Seneca, Lancelot, Baudit, Spot, Fido, Butch, Hamish, Henry, Silver, Lightening,
Nathan, Woody, Gretchen, Jane, Blaze Furey, Hochidann, Mike, Stagel, Cheebee, Sir, Tar Tar,
Ralph, Becky, Thursday, Aristotle, Russell, Dusty, Ned, Fidel, Silver Jimminy, Bugler, Streak,
Jesse, Skipper, Cricket, Hex, Schniepf, Fridolin, Wuli, Pip, Beebop, Burpee, Putzchen, Ruby,
Dog, Ruff, Schroeder, Snoopy, Ferpo, Chuzzie, Sunshine, Chukka, Lucky, Quinn, Red, Big,
Singer, Fenwick, Scruffy, Toledo, Marvin, Frou Frou, Biege on Baby, Moose Cow J. Jones,
Tiny, Duke, Downie, Sadie, Mississippi, Samuel J. Pugsley, Manchester Guardian, Oreo,
Thank You, Tramp, Samson, Cardinal Woolsey, Belinda, Happy, Lassie, Woof, Stinker,
Jessica, Marko, Cloud, Dignity, Payday, Igor Graff, Happy Boy, Buck, Molly, Strider, Chuck,
Samson, Bruno, Rube, Mickey, Lance, Rasputin, Sabra, Bob, Odd, Flame, Dakota, Arfy,
Barky, Pal, Good, Lasa, Jerry, Precious, Maurizio, Fred, Thalin, Junior, Siegfried, Fritz,
Sinbad, Henderson, Robby, Flash, Moon, Keller, Bitsy, Pooh, Ch. Ingo v. Wunschelrute,
Piggy, MacGregor, Daisy, Toby, O'Brien, Wolf, Snip, Dorcas, Sam Roberts, Troubador, Fang,
Pepe La Knute, Roscoe, Plato, Luke, Star, Devvy, Mutt, George, Bella, Babette, Gus, Brutus,
Sheba, Jefferson, Horace, Slave, Stony, Mush, Maybe, Rollo, Marmaduke, Jasper, Bowser,
Tubby, Amanda Belle, Gemini, Pepi, Sonny, Tiger, Marshall, Ready, Ginger, Lady-bug, Curry,
Holly, Dolly, Happy Annie, Golden Boy, Samuel J. Penny, Sarg, Pugsley, Lola, Tulip, Marvin,
Paddy, Dunsan, Sport, Genevieve, Captain, Mittens, Attaboy, Mr. Payday, Casey, Doughboy,
Moro, Satan, Pride, Hamlet, Tinder Reb, Blue, Sonny, Soupy, Tricksy, Come, Speed, Vet,
Singer, Dobin, Hilda, Lanyard II, Higgens, Killer, Oslo, Sleeper, Cuddles, Sadie, Gabby T
Bone, Snowball, Penelope, Otto, Senior, Chien, Chipps, Bonny, Sidecar, Amigo, Buck,
Denver, Aries, Chops, Lucretia, Adam, Leonardo, Pansy, Solo, Speed, Casper, Freida, Pacer,

About My Friends
by
P.G. Wodehouse

We all have plenty to say about dogs, but very seldom are we allowed to say it. One of the familiar sights at any cocktail party is that of a man—call him Man A—trying to tell another man—call him Man B—all about the intelligence of his dog and the other man cutting in and starting to tell him all about the intelligence of *his* dog; whereupon Man A raises his voice and Man B raises his voice until both are bringing plaster down from the ceiling and giving bystanders the impression that they have wandered into a student protest demonstration. It is estimated by statisticians that more pique, umbrage, dudgeon, and bad blood are engendered in this way than by any other method of engendering p, u, d, and bb. True, blows are seldom exchanged, but these encounters nearly always lead to the ending of friendships.

How wise, then, of Mr. Elliott Erwitt to avoid those vulgar brawls and stick to photographing dogs instead of talking about them. No agony for him of being shouted down by some uncouth moron with a louder voice. And what superb photographs his are. It does one good to look at them. There is not a sitter in his gallery who does not melt the heart. And no beastly class distinctions, either. Thoroughbred or mutts, they are all here.

What with one thing and another it was not till I went to live at Great Neck, Long Island, that I actually owned a dog of my own. Guy Bolton, Jerry Kern and I were writing a revue for Flo Ziegfeld at that time. It did only thirty-seven performances, so the pickings were none too good, but I was able to save something out of the wreck, for one of the company gave me a French bulldog called Sammy, as amiable and sweet-natured an animal as ever broke biscuit. Too amiable, we sometimes used to feel. He was always liking the looks of passers-by outside our garden gate and trotting out to fraternize with them. The first time he disappeared I gave the man who brought him back ten dollars, and this got around among the local children and stirred up their business instincts. They would come to our gate and call, "Sammy, Sammy, Sammy," and old Sam would waddle along and they would bring him back with a cheery "We found your dog wandering down the road, mister," and cash in. Obviously no purse could stand the drain, especially with revues running for only thirty-seven performances. The bottom dropped out of the market, and it was not long before any child who collected a quarter thought he had done well.

When Sammy succumbed to old age, I made what I think was a mistake by appointing as his successor an Aberdeen terrier who was supposed (though he seldom did) to answer to the name of Angus. Aberdeen terriers are intelligent and (if you don't mind those beetling eyebrows) handsome, but so austere and full of the Calvinistic spirit that it is impossible for an ordinary erring human being not to feel ill at ease in their presence. Angus had a way of standing in front of me and looking at me like a Scottish preacher about to rebuke the sins of his congregation. Sundays with him were particularly trying. There is almost nothing you can do on a Sunday which does not arouse the disapproval of an Aberdeen terrier. He would grudgingly consent to come with me for a walk after lunch, but if I so forgot myself as to whistle for him, his manner

plainly showed what his opinion was of people so sunk in sin as to whistle on the Sabbath. It was a relief when I gave him to a better man than myself.

After Angus my wife and I fell under the spell of Pekes. Many people, I know, disparage Pekes, but take it from me, they are all right. If they have a fault, it is a tendency to think too much of themselves. One can readily understand it, of course. For centuries they belonged only to Emperors. If you were not an Emperor and were found with a Peke on your premises, you got the Death Of A Thousand Cuts, an old Chinese punishment for minor offenses roughly equivalent to our fifteen-dollar fine for parking next to a fire plug. But none of our Pekes pulled rank on us. They could not have been more democratic and affable. And how Mr. Elliott Erwitt would have loved to photograph them.

Over Bill the foxhound, the first of our Remsenburg dogs, even Mr. Erwitt, broadminded though he is, would, I'm afraid, have shaken his head. Bill was a stray in the last stages of starvation and so covered with ticks that only the keenest eye could detect that there was a dog underneath.

Taken in and fed and nursed and scientifically de-ticked, he soon settled down—but only in the country. Came a time when he had to come with us to New York, when, alighting from the car, he refused to enter the apartment house, evidently suspecting a trap. I dragged him as far as the elevator, and again he jibbed. I finally got him on board, and he then refused to emerge. No doubt he thought that while conditions in the elevator were pretty bad, they were nothing to the horrors which lurked behind that sinister apartment door. The whole thing was very like the big scene in one of those old movies where the prison personnel are trying to persuade James Cagney to enter the death chamber. Eventually, after many days, he decided his fears had been ill-founded and we were all able to relax.

The question of whether dogs have a sense of humor is often hotly debated, and I should like to take it up with Mr. Erwitt next time he has a moment. My own opinion is that some have and some don't. Dachshunds have, but not St. Bernards and Great Danes. It would seem that a dog

has to be small to be fond of a joke. You never find an Irish wolfhound trying to be a stand-up comic.

But it is fatal to let any dog know that he is funny, for he immediately loses his head and starts hamming it up. As an instance of this I would point to Rudolph, a dachshund I once owned, whose slogan was Anything for a Laugh. Dachshunds are always the worst offenders in this respect because of their peculiar shape. It is only natural that when a dog finds that his mere appearance makes the viewing public giggle, he should assume that Nature intended him for a comedian's role.

I had a cottage at the time outside an English village, not far from a farm where they kept ducks, and one day the farmer called on me to say his ducks were disappearing and suspicion had fallen on my Rudolph. Why? I asked, and he said because mine was the only dog in the vicinity except his own Towser, and Towser had been so carefully trained that he would not touch a duck if you brought it to him with orange sauce over it.

I was indignant. I said he had only to gaze into Rudolph's candid brown eyes to see how baseless were his suspicions. Had he not, I asked, heard of foxes? Or weasels? Or stoats? How much more likely that one of these was the Bad Guy in the sequence? He was beginning to waver and seemed on the verge of an apology, when Rudolph, who had been listening with the greatest interest and at a certain point had left the room, came troting in with a duck in his mouth.

Yes, dachshunds overplay their sense of humor, and I suppose other dogs have their defects, but they seem trivial compared with their merits. So put down that camera, Mr. Erwitt, and join me in a standing ovation to all dogs, whether Airedales, wire-haired terriers, bulldogs, Pekinese, Cairns, spaniels, pugs, Maltese, Yorkshires, borzois, bloodhounds, Bedlingtons, pointers, setters, mastiffs, Newfoundlands, St. Bernards, Great Danes, collies, chows, poodles, and those peculiar little Mexican dogs beginning with C and sounding like a sneeze.

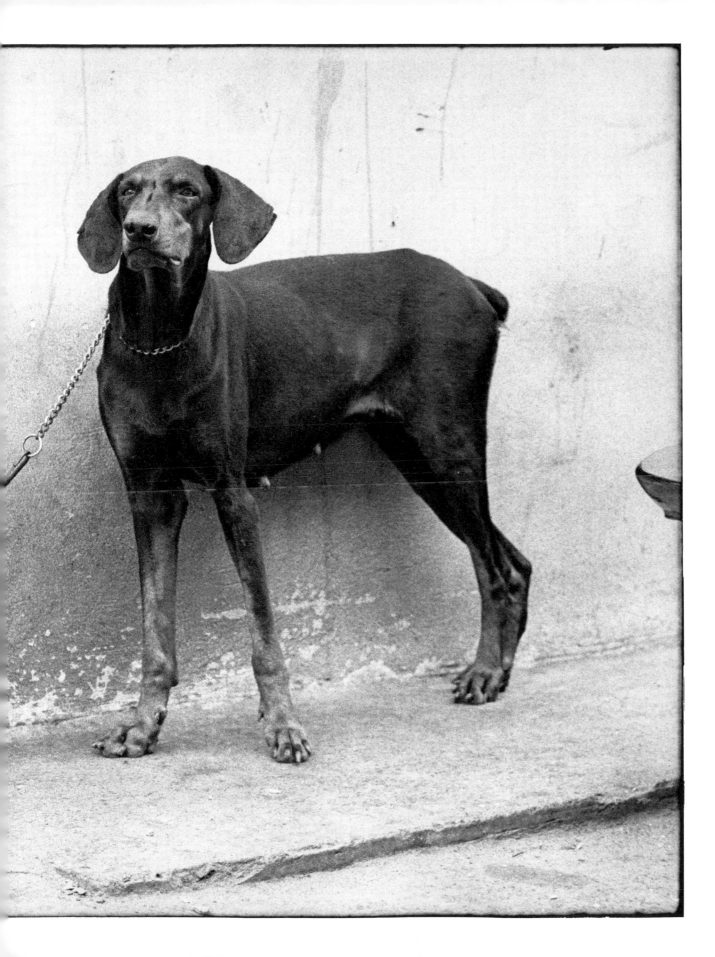

28

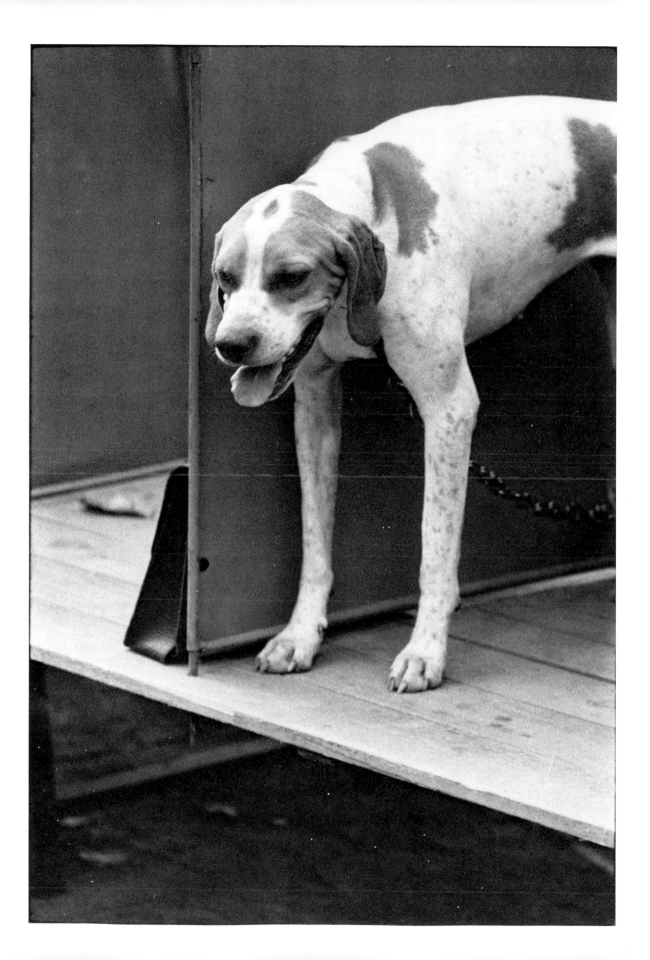

LIST OF ILLUSTRATIONS

Introduction sequence, Paris, 1952